Sugar Lumps
and
Black Eye Blues

TS Hawkins

iUniverse, Inc.
Bloomington

I am like an old forgotten piano waiting to be fine tuned|sitting alone desperately longing for someone to lend a helping hand|rusted, scratched eternally from being undiscovered|wishing that someone would unleash the musical essence lurking inside so the world would realize how wonderful I am| I am like an old forgotten piano waiting to be fine tuned|sitting alone desperately longing for someone to lend a helping hand|rusted, scratched eternally from being undiscovered|wishing that someone would unleash the musical essence lurking inside so the world would realize how wonderful I am| I am like an old forgotten piano waiting to be fine tuned|sitting alone desperately longing for someone to lend a helping hand|rusted, scratched eternally from being undiscovered|wishing that someone would unleash the musical essence lurking inside so the world would realize how wonderful I am| I am like an old forgotten piano waiting to be fine tuned|sitting alone desperately longing for someone to lend a helping hand|rusted. scratched eternally from being undiscovered|wishing that someone would unleash the musical essence lurking inside so the world would realize how wonderful I am|I am like an old forgotten piano waiting to be fine tuned|sitting alone desperately longing for someone to lend a helping hand|rusted. scratched eternally from being undiscovered|wishing that someone would unleash the musical essence lurking inside so the world would realize how wonderful I am| I am like an old forgotten piano waiting to be fine tuned|sitting alone desperately longing for someone to lend a helping hand|rusted. scratched eternally from being undiscovered|wishing that someone would unleash the musical essence lurking inside so the world would realize how wonderful I am|I am like an old forgotten piano waiting to be fine tuned|sitting alone desperately longing for someone to lend a helping hand|rusted. scratched eternally from being undiscovered|wishing that someone would unleash the musical essence lurking inside so the world would realize how wonderful I am|I am like an old forgotten piano waiting to be fine tuned|sitting alone desperately longing for someone to lend a helping hand|rusted, scratched eternally from being undiscovered| wishing that someone

Sugar Lumps and Black Eye Blues

OTHER TITLES BY TS HAWKINS

***

Confectionately Yours
Mahogany Nectar
Lil Blæk Book: All the Long Stories Short
The Hotel Haikus
Running Still Water

UPCOMING RELEASES
Black Suga: diary of a troublesome teenager
Poetry Schmo-etry
A Woman Scorned is a Woman Blessed
On My Knees Too Long: Prayers, Proverbs & Poems to GOD
Becoming Saturn: Counting Backwards from 60-30

Books/CDs available for purchase at all major online retailers
&
www.tspoetics.com

ACKNOWLEDGEMENTS

***

...a journey unforeseen...

DEDICATION

***

Dorothy
Charlese
Eloise
Nana
Kimmika
Keisha

The Lakewood Chapter of New Jersey Orators

The "240" Family

MENU OF MOMENTS

***

DESSERT: *Servin' It Up and Thinkin' It Over*

B.Y.O.B

a forward by Kimmika LH Williams-Witherspoon, PhD

***

Sugar Lumps and Black Eye Blues is the clever, contemporary and memorable debut work of Hawkins; now known in the poetry circuit as TS Hawkins. Chronicling the joy in growing into adulthood and the, sometimes, pain of (as she writes *In the Midst of Sorrow*) being "loved to death", Hawkins' work, crystallizes one young woman's journey but speaks to all women about identity and our search for "filling".

As the book's divisions or, as she calls them, *Menu of Moments* suggests, the poems in this collection prove to be the "food" that has comforted this young author's soul. Gracious and generous, in **Sugar Lumps and Black Eye Blues**, she prepares a table for her readers from the work that has provided "food for comfort" for her all these many years of her young "20-something" life.

Honest, open, sometimes "boiling hot", "come as you are", "down-home", B.Y.O.B.—some of the pain and tribulations that are main ingredients in her work can be "searing". The moments and stories that the author creates will, no doubt, hang heavy on your consciousness and your emotional pallet, as they will be hard to forget once the book is down and the initial "read" is done. You will, nevertheless, be drawn to Hawkins' table again and again to appreciate the depth of experience in her work. Certainly, you will, I'm sure, savor the imagery in the unmistakable "twist" on language lines that are uniquely hers.

There's double entendre in poems like *Impurities*, where she ruminates about identity "white on the inside". Her work incorporates "mind-boggling" prose in lines like: "I want to be the eraser shavings that held your mistakes" in *If Only I Could Write Like You*. Poems like *A Christmas Moment* are cute and charming and make powerful statements about duplicity and political economy while still making you smile; and no one captures the "risqué" in love-making like Hawkins' can in *Only You Can*. And, yes...I hazard to guess that

every reader will take long moments to pause and ponder poems like *Reflection of Your Rejection* with Hawkins' powerful lines like:
"emotional wounds/
make tombs/
that Jesus can't even move over."

Without a doubt, the most painful poems in Hawkins' collection are also the most passionate; but as we know from life's lessons in hell's kitchen, sometimes even when the "food" is scorched, it can still be good and "good for us".

As she continues to make a name for herself as a poet/performer/author, **Sugar Lumps and Black Eye Blues** will surely be a "must-have" addition to every bibliophile's collection!

UNDERSTANDING THE LUMPS
an introduction
***

As a young girl, my mother used to sit in the corner for hours lost in the wonders of books. She would conjure up dreams and methods of escape from her everyday struggles. Being the fifth of nine in a single parent household due to the early death of her father and not having her life handed to her on a silver platter, books became her compass to map routes of reality.

I, like my mother, longed for escape. Not because I unhappy, but I needed to seek understanding and a sense of security. At seven years old, I juggled the divorce of my parents, a move to a new town, a new baby sister and becoming second in command before developing a sense of self. To mask anxiety, poetry became an outlet for me. The writings of others spoke to me in ways my parents never could. Such images from the works of Robert Frost (**The Road Not Taken** and **The Lockless Door**) and Nikki Giovanni (**Woman Poem** and **How Do You Write A Poem?**) comforted me as I worked on finding a voice for myself.

Decades between us, my mother and I had one thing in common; words. She read them while I wrote them to ease woes. Poetry became my accent to speak of tales, observations and various unbelievable moments. **Sugar Lumps and Black Eye Blues** serves as that observation of life, a journal of emotions and a revelation of self and others. Each piece highlights a quest of understanding love, lust and lessons through the eyes of a budding woman. **Sugar Lumps and Black Eye Blues**, blueprints mental and emotional connections that may have been lost in daily tasks or events that have been shielded by the veil of the subconscious. The overall goal, of the book, is to mend the past to foster a promising future in all aspects of relationship. In taking time to savor the vulnerable delicacies, you may find a piece of your own truth.

I encourage you to "break fast" from the routine of the everyday. Find a comfortable spot to dibble and dabble , loosen your belt loop to laugh, cry, lick your fingers and tap your feet to the entrée's I serve.

Whatever suits your fancy, just decide to enjoy each moment and I hope to see you for seconds!

MOMMA'S WORRY
a prologue
***

Tell me…
Tell me anything
Tell me anything but this news breaking headline
Tell me…
Tell me anything

Tell me you overslept
Due to late night partying
Turning tricks
Doing third shifts of boozing
When books were supposed to be your only focus
Tell me you were on the phone
Conversing with your estranged father
Filling him in about the salty dreams
I wiped away every night since your youth
Tell me you were studying biology
Betwixt her labia
Highlighting orgasmic vocabulary
Creating jealous retinas
For they didn't develop a photographic memory
To scan questioning sexuality
…but I secretly knew you we're gay…
Tell me that the one night stand
Lain you down for breakfast in bed
Nourishing your belly with lies of new beginning
Dismantling the foundation I've created for you
Flatbacking common sense for a trollup
Whose only mission was to pony around with your emotions

Tell me…
Tell me anything
Tell me anything but this news breaking headline
Tell me…
Tell me anything

Tell me lies of working late
Volunteering to take more shifts
Knowing you never filled out your work-study paperwork
Nor got up off your ass to apply for a real part time job
Tell me you were at the beach
Surfing for excuses of why financial aid never received the tuition check
I placed in your backpack
Tell me that your roommates weed had you two puffs and passed out
For three days
Laced with your experimented naivety
Smoke beaming of an herbal essence
Is the only reason you couldn't respond to me
Tell me your cell phone was stolen
Tell me your computer only works in safe mode
Tell me the bursar disconnected the LAN-line for unpaid bills
Tell me the university internet system was yielded for repairs

Baby, please tell me you tried to reach me today…

Tell me you're not there
Gallivanting
School skipping to find the hotdog vendor they now call ground 0
That number can't register in my mind
As you were turning 18 today
Tell me you're not there
Cheating my opportunity to acknowledge your birth alone
Sharing our private moments with the commercialism of destruction
Tell me that's not your plane
Descending
Glass ceiling crashing its way onto my television screen
Tell me those limbs and shrapnel aren't the creations of my womb
Tell me the black box didn't serve as the umbilical cord
Giving you live through death
Tell me those buildings aren't tucking you into sleep
Where screams and sirens become lullabies

Tell me…
Tell me anything

Tell me anything but this news breaking headline
Tell me...
Tell me anything

Baby, tell me you tried to reach me today...

Tell me the secretary didn't write the message down
Tell me my phone battery died
Had no signal
Went to voicemail
Tell me I don't have to remember you when everyone else does
Tell me that your last photo
Isn't a redneck bumper sticker
Sloganning *"We'll Never Forget"*
Your brown eyes
Now red, white, blue artillery looking back at me
Tell me this makeshift grave isn't yours
Where you and the rising death toll bear one name
Tell me you weren't a pawn in Bush's revenge
Check
Mate
Becoming middle-class war bait
Changing thousands of birthdates to 9-11

Tell me...
Tell me anything
Tell me anything but this news breaking headline
Tell me...
Tell me anything

Cocktails & Appetizers

The Beginning

Tuned Out

I am
Like an old forgotten piano
Waiting to be fine tuned
Sitting alone
Desperately longing
For someone to lend a helping hand
Rusted and scratched eternally
From being undiscovered
Wishing that someone would unleash
The musical essence lurking inside
So the world would realize how wonderful
I am

Blind Iris

A ticking time bomb
Soiled in regret, pain; agony
Defeat hadn't completely stolen her soul
Worked for years finding her niche
Not realizing she was great all by herself
Emotionally flammable
Wore her heart on her sleeve
Always giving the love that she is in search for

Epitaph

Perfume eulogy
Scented masquerade harpoon casket forget-me-nots
Rose petal goodbyes
Unlock an afterlife practiced in secret

Unmarked Grave

In my flesh ridden
Tomb, I consume you daily
And you don't notice

In my flesh ridden
Tomb, I consume you daily
And you don't notice

Lying in a space of God's creation
Six feet under circumstances
Greed, self-pity, trials and love
A rigor mortis moment in time
She lies here
Hopefully finding the peace
That she was searching for
A daughter, a sister, a niece, a granddaughter, a lover
Too many who needed it
But much of nothing to herself

I consume you daily
And you don't notice

Note 2 Self

Everything never wanted was all that was needed
Moonlit dancing on horizoned truth
Come home to the stranger that should have been the one;
for someone's else
Had I waited, would you've come?

<u>Hopeful</u>

Prance to the beat of your unborn breath
Await to taste;
delve in your splendor

No Red, No White; Just Two Blue Lines

In order to live
The American Dream, I
sacrificed my child

Twice, without the choice
Disgrace would grace the eyes that
granted my soul life

<u>Reminisce</u>

Shard organs
Remind the mind
To mind the memories

Futuristic Planning

Premeditated goals
Ambitions caught up in a one night stand;
denial
Avoid silver lining by wadding
in shallow streams of consciousness

I Am What I Am

I am disaster
I wonder what they see in me
I hear the positivity spewed at me, but all
I see is that
I am disaster

I pretend not to concede to hurt
I feel inadequate
I touch my soul to ensure that the flesh is alive
I worry that no one will take the time to do the same, for
I am disaster

I understand that there has to be a light at the end of the tunnel
I say "Lord hear my plea"
I dream of soaring above the suffrage
I try to ignore the urge to be invective to my spirit
I hope to succeed, though I still believe that
I am disaster

Impurities

Eats the underwear
Cleans the floor
The countertops;
My mind
To punish it
I drank it
It retaliated
Punished me
Through cleansing the impurities
It was one
Knocking me unconscious
Lying there helpless
Unsure of why
I thought that was how you become white on the inside

...I was always being accused of it...

Journey

Broad and Susquehanna
Cecil B. Moore
Girard
Fairmount
Traveled to Spring Garden
But no evidence of the latter
Up the stairs to 17th street
A bar and a black man that couldn't pass it
Greet me…
smile at me…
bring fear to me…
Yet I stay
Walk in duo to his place;
cavern of uncertainty
Unlock the door the to this personal prison
The fragrant man smell pierces my nostrils
While he penetrates me
unwillingly
Drinks not the cause
True answers unknown
Realizing that the smell of man
No longer smells sweet to me

Love Touches

She holds me
Fresh
Clean
Dripping wet from the sink
Towel not completely doing its job
Decoration
I coo
She smiles
Our bond
One of many
Enjoyable
Refreshing
Soothing
A daily repetition
[*I don't mind*]
She holds me
Fresh
Clean
Dripping wet from the sink
Towel not completely doing its job
Decoration
I coo
She smiles
Our bond
Ritual
One of many

The First

Water
Wave
Wonder
Whet
Willingly rock
Sway yesses on my nape
To remind me it's but a dream

Many Thanks

Walk with my head up
Not due to arrogance
Not due to conceitedness
Not due to haughtiness
But because
I worked hard to be somebody

No Interruptions

Searching for the onyx dream
Continually live in a maze
Zigzagging;
scurrying in a haste to end up no place
Non-existent you are
Not knowing this spend years,
lifetimes
eternities to remain hopeless
I tire
No longer shoving the soul into a false sense of security
Surrendering what's left to an unmarked grave
Destiny unforeseen
A story of
Sugared lumps
and black eye blues

Entrées

Wrapped Present Memories

If Only I Could Write Like You

You amaze me every time you step up to the mic
The oceans' bottom can't compete
Because you are so deep
Would do anything just to be close to the words that you spit
Want to be the eraser shavings that held your mistakes
Your computer typos
Your pen scribbling
The drop of hot sauce that dripped from the greasy chicken
You had for lunch on the subway ride to class
While writing your poetry homework assignment
Because it was able to touch your page
Want to be your last minute thoughts
Your brain farts
Your performance stumbles
Anything to be next to your genius
Can you cry under water?
So that one day
I could taste your wisdom
Through the tap water of my poetic uncertainty
The visual projections that shine through your rhyme
Answer the question of can blind people see in their dreams
Hell yes,
Your iambic pentameter
Is the music that sings on in their subconscious
You dazzle me
If I wasn't weighted down
I'd be swept off my feet
Somehow you send me on a rollercoaster journey
That will exercise my mental state
Lose emotional pounds from your words
Can I take a class in your poetic madness?
My poetry is even hard for me to decipher
Even after writing this
I feel inadequate
Would do anything just to be your mediocre
So I can have a fair chance

An Ode to The Past

Takes me back
Takes me back to the playground
Where grass tickles the toes and hands touch clean sand in sandboxes
Mother's snacks placed in a diaper bag that I was too old for
But I didn't care
My momma loved me
As she watched me play
Living and loving life
The sun beats down on me
Just like she would
If I didn't come-a-runnin' by the second time she called my name
But I was too busy
Busy bobbing on seesaws
Swinging on swings and whirling on the big toy thing
That could have you spinning in circles for hours
As your mind vomits from being dizzy
You stand up and do it again
because you subconsciously love the feeling

Takes me back
Takes me back where grass tickles the toes in a playground
Where I was once safe
People looked out for me then
Blanketed my fears with a pallet of comfort and joy
But times have changed
I dread life because it is no longer a game
Dwelling in a world where societal norms seesaw
Tossing emotions back and forth
Battling my creditability by the fickle standards of this nation
Being judged because being black and swinging both ways is taboo;
strike two
Whirling around in the sea of confusion
I am the future

I want to go back
Back to a time
Where my only concern was touching clean sand in sandboxes

Where grass tickles the toes lulling me into serenity as I play
And eating mother's snacks
Placed in a diaper bag that I was too old for
But I didn't care
I saw how much my momma loved me
As she watched me play
Living and loving life

Funkytown

Day breaks me
As I slip on pajama pants
Causing back to ache
No time to address the pain
'cuz I'm running late
Showering with shampoo
Ain't no more body wash left
"Shouldn't have bought that drink last night"
Air drying
Vagina blowing in the wind
No clean towels
No time to address the frustration
'cuz I'm running late
In route to train station
Fell down steps
New jeans no longer new
Still missed the 8:45am
Train that runs every 8 minutes…
10 minutes late
Surprised at the smooth transfer
I took a sigh of relief
Next train comes
Find non-moist seat
Collect my thoughts and wait for my stop
2nd and Market
Conductor says
"NEXT STOP, 13th STREET"
Doors open
Ease lifted by an odoriferous element
A man
Six feet with a bald head nearly skimming the train ceiling
Entering at approximately 950 pounds…
Minimum
Sits in the seat next to mine
"Isn't there a three-seater he could take advantage of?"
Both not skinny people
He should have known better

Whining to self
"I was here first"
Sealing the deal
Mashed into this space while a smell wallops my nostrils
Nose hairs ablaze from funk
Emanating from the pores he missed
Cringing
Shoving my face into the corner
Praying his stop was on its way
No time to weep
'cuz I'm running late
His stop came
Thanked all spirits
Unfurled myself from the crouched position
Eased into a lean
Only to hear the conductor say
"NEXT STOP, FRANKFORD"
WWHHAATT!!!!!!,
Are you kidding me?
That fat
funky pore ridden fuck
Made me hibernate to the ends of Philadelphia
No time to kick his ass
'cuz I'm running late
For work

Reflection of Your Rejection

I'm a reflection of your rejection
Hating because I do you
Better than you could ever conceive
You better believe that there's more to come
Through sipping your venomous libation
Tired of your continuous degradation of my soul
You're swole,
That the things they tried to change in you
Are the things they love in me
Sick of putting you on this elevation
As you climb to continue to push me down
Because you see me a reflection of your rejection
Drained from living this falsified perfection
So I am trying to get diesel
The fuel you are feeding me is lethal
Desperate need of a resurrection
Your emotional wounds make tombs that Jesus can't move over
Just step back,
You're all fiction; no facts
And I'm weary from absorbing all your slack

In The Midst Of Sorrow: A Revelation

Can't make you love me
If you don't
But I remember when you told me you did
Later taking it back
Claiming it to be love just *for me*
Yet I stayed
Allowed you to pitch a tent of false security inside me
Camp there for hours
Hoping that you'd learn to love me
I know of nothing else
Bringing suffering to myself
Like an emancipated slave
With no freedom papers to unhitch my bondage
Mentally shackled
Emotionally tired from the lies you feed me
Like a snake to its prey
Squeezed so tightly that survival means death
Consume all of your venom
I know of nothing more
You continue to use me
I continue to stay
Both at fault; not one willing to escape from the shadow of denial
Conditioned myself to believe that I am worthless
Without worth
Without you
In this credo
Found comfort in your abrasive embrace
Your touch; sandpaper scraping
Filing away my joy
Your eyes grip my soul
Tightly squeezing my aura
Can't make a stifling cry
Tremble with fear when you hold me
In one rapid blink
Black and blue bruises highlight my vision
Your territory
Once again marked

Kisses assure me that it would be the last time
This time
So I stay
My forehead
Your lips
Small lancets that tear me into shards
Even if pieced together
They wouldn't resemble my being
Look for change
Another bruise emerges
Unsure if I want to survive
Because maybe
Just maybe
If I knew me well enough
To love me just enough
Wouldn't have become accustomed
To letting you love me
To death

<u>In Search</u>

In search for regularity
Try to cleanse the hatred
That floods the crevices of my mind
Unsure why
You're the one that really fucked up
Fucked up so bad you fucked me up
All because you wanted to fuck
And I told you NO
All I have is this emotional bulimia
Hording everything inside
Until I can find a sheet of paper to spew thoughts
Constantly looking for purity between white lines
To mask the black ink blotches that I claim as emotions
You cloud my sanity
Becoming the fog that continues to block my senses,
Senses that no longer sense my sense of self
Smell
Feel
Taste you
Every minute
Of every day
Want it to stop
Like a predator to prey
Hovering over my existence
Plotting the destruction of my salvation
Stop stalking me
Stop fucking stalking me
What I want to yell to you
Tears stifle demands
Only they can be heard as I cry to sleep
Weep into unconsciousness
Mind vomits answers to answerless questions
All I am able to purge
You made a fool of me
Tell me why
I have emerged from greatness
Legacy

Where my lap is throne
From which your lineage is formed
Without my support
Your domain will never reign supreme
Why I am still nothing in your eyes?
Vision of my crown and glory
Rusted from all you've done to me
Rewrote me
In just one moment
You stole my joy
Ability to love
My sanity
My trust
My dignity
All in one fucking moment
Castrated my soul with vigorous pounding on sealed territory
Stabbing phallic flags in places that didn't belong to you
Each thrust
I bellow
Your hazardous materials melt away my essence
Rot
Inside out
Lying in a puddle of "NO's",
Only thing that rings clear
You made a fool of me
Tell me why
Allowed your homicidal tendencies
To glock- nine with my mental state
Thought that being alone would hurt me the most
You portrayed yourself as being the man that would make a difference
The difference was that you were no different
A mere child in the suit of a man
Who believes that two drinks seal sexual contracts that only one of us
Had the opportunity to sign
No negotiation
Just pressured
Forced into submission
Treating me less than your equal
Downsizing my humanity

Slave to your insecurity of power
I did nothing to deserve this
Yet
You made a fool of me
Tell me why

Fiery's Paintbrushes

As red as the crimson stream flowing within you,
serves as a venomous libation
I wallow in your aqueous solution, seeping into my pores
Becoming bluer than the longing eyes seeking freedom
through the windows of depression

Fucking just to be fucked
Galvanized in your cum, sticking to your phallic floor
As red as the crimson stream flowing within you,
serves as a venomous libation

I am still being fucked just to be fucked, a rut
Going insane looking inside you for more
Becoming bluer than the longing eyes seeking freedom
through the windows of depression

Doggishly styled fucked, missionary
"I ain't no nun fucked"; emotional smut
Caramelized in your hatred, armless fingers reaching for the door
As red as the crimson stream flowing within you,
serves as a venomous libation

I keep drinking, drinking, drinking drunk while acids in my gut
Vomit, spewing through the soul with this elongated tour
Becoming bluer than the longing eyes seeking freedom
through the windows of depression

I am still being fucked to be fucked
Galvanized in your cum, sticking to your phallic floor
As red as the crimson stream flowing within you,
serves as a venomous libation, I
Become bluer than the longing eyes seeking freedom
through the windows of depression

Come Save Me

Home
Long to be where I can use the word again
A place where joy eases angst
Cradle long-lasting memories
that resemble the groundwork that I see in others
This decadent temple housing my fortitude
is no longer useful to me
Tired of the dismay seeping from the ceiling
Drenching carpets of despair,
Molding the woodwork of confusion
I live here
Constantly dwelling in infestation
No sweet sorrows
Just endless tomorrows and pain
Shattered
Torn up
from the floor boards
Societal fumigators raid subconscious
Linger amongst the waste
Grow weary waiting for salvation
Someone
Anyone
Save me

More Than a Rendezvous

Can't look me in the eye
Can you
Do you love living your lie?

Gazing deeply
As the sun sets on an empty orifice you call a soul
Fabricated tissues imitating a fleshy shell
Masking reality with the stench of your denial
You've succumb to repetitious actions eluding cosmetic comfort
Brimstone raging flames screaming to be set free
Symbolizing the truth you won't devour
Promenading fallacies
Sweetly colored and laced in the stitching of the umbrella you carry
A high rise soap box
Merely a stain on your white gloved insecurities
Pretentiously masturbating society into believing your deceit
Making them secrete
Venomous cum
Completely mind fucked by your trickery
Complicating the ones who know true love regardless of form
But you are suave
Smooth talking
Allowing others to believe you are common
Ejaculating your fiction betwixt my fingers
I lapped the tale dry
Mourning the residue
It's the closest I can get to you
Yet still can't pretend that part of me does not exist
My magic is not as strong as yours

Can't look me in the eye
Can you
Do you love living your lie?

Writhing in agony
Stop posting your guilt with self-hatred thorns inside me
Dwelling in your tickle dick tragedy

Ever considered how I felt
How can you resurrect ones soul?
Wallow in the blessing
Encase it back into the tomb
And tell it to wait for another miracle
You didn't mean to save me
Screwed me six ways to Sunday
Never to rise again
Looked to you as my healer
Surprisingly denied the revolutions
to relieve this Jack-in-the-box
That was the problem
I am and you are a Jill
Tumbling, tumbling, tumbling until…
Smashed back into the plastic cell
Confined to the dark spaces of your mind
Bars barricading four cornered illusions
Awaiting a childlike innocence
Trust
An entity I no longer see
Blurred visions masquerading as confusion
Blinded by your inconsistencies

Can't look me in the eye
Can you
Do you love living your lie?

Time ticking away
Molasses minutes piling more questions
That slit wrists can no longer answer
Emotions tangled in your essence
Leaving me breathless
Wishing to stress less
But I am all wound up
Alarmed by the twisted dance we did
To some degree still do
Can't shake this uneasy feeling
Watching you prostitute other connections to avoid my gaze
STOP

Take a moment to capture my existence
Titanically, seeking rationale from your cerebral blueprint
You've become the pollutant that won't sieve from my body
Penetrated so deeply
Rotting my roots
Ceasing sprouts of clarity
I need not suffer anymore
But you

Can't look me in the eye
Can you
Do you love living your lie?

Without me

Package

Abruptly you appeared into my life when I was
Battling the true meaning of myself, I
Cower that you might be interested in what I have to offer
Detriment circles my mind as your
Emotions embrace my spirit. A
Fear of committing to you; dedicated to self-destruction, please
God, this package is wrapped in the reflective image of me
Help me understand why we move to the same
Iambic pentameter as we
Join together in the hammock of life
Kindred spirits that have finally crossed paths
Linked to each other's soul, you
Masturbate my thoughts
Numbing my speech to vibrations resonating through the
Orifices of my lips
Penetrating honey dipped crevices of you claimed as my territory. Still
Questioning every moment and emotion, I need
Rationale because I'm
Scared; I have become accustomed to living in suffrage and viewed as
Tainted soil; trying to logically
Understand what you see in me
Virtually confused about this dance we do
Waiting for divine answers, I settle for
Xerox print outs of joy I once had
Yielding for the chance to be in your
Zone, though you are a package wrapped in the reflective image of me

Sugar Lumps and Black Eye Blues

"CD's and DVD's and CD's and DVD's
CD's and DVD's" and…

Saw you
SEPTA train peddler
Searching for a 9 to 5 through an electronic hustle
You glared at me
I glared at you
And I glared at we,
Thought you were sweet
In the moment
Selling those 1 for $5 or 3 for $10
Then,
You sat next to me
Remembering I ain't had none in a week
I let you speak
Caught up in your rhythm and rhyme
The dreams you might find
Letting ears linger in your thoughts
Let my eyes do the talking
As my smile made pathway to your emotions
For your small attempt at devotion
Remembering I ain't had none in a week
Loins began to tweak
Almost sprung a leak
So, let you continue to speak
All the days and weeks to follow
Still believing you were sweet
In the moment
Escaping in your mantra

"CD's and DVD's and CD's and DVD's
CD's and DVD's" and…

Is that all you do
Trying to think back as to why I thought that was cute
Days ain't running as smooth as anticipated

No schematics to blueprint dreams
Plans not laid yet I am, everyday
Watching you plummet into hollow comfort
While I labor
Paying bills
Doing housework
Satisfying your needs
As your feet get cemented in greed and
Deceit, leading to arguments
Where for me there is no retreat
Stretching thin of what's left of me
You continue to beg for more
And not wanting loneliness again
Second job I acquire to fill a void
To avoid aggravations
Sucked in a whirlwind of endless cycles
1 job, 2 job, dinner dishes, blowjob
1 job, 2 job, dirty dishes, blowjob
1 job, 2 job, do the dishes, blowjob
Routinely circumcising brain waves
Washed up in madness, leaving only sadness
On both sides
Thus you stick by
Not by love
But by benefit
Until I decided to quit
That's the first time you hit
Slit face from lobe to cheek
With ring I bought, never noticing I was meek
Allowing your digits to do the persuading
Because you are annoyed at dead end prospects
Non job hunting
Weed absorbing leech
With a speech using lies to justify slothful stride
Lured into serenity
Cuddling false security
Knowing it's only about the money
Tolerating me until it disappears
What to do to get more cash

So face won't get smashed
Complementing other wounds; forgetting them there
Sometimes
Until the new ones come
Can't believe I'm the one
Educated...
Strong willed...
Determined...
It hurts to be the one mocked
Pretending ignorance
Standing in sinking sands of nothingness
With partner's worthlessness
Contemplating on how it began
It was him
SEPTA train peddler
Searching for a 9 to 5 with an electronic hustle
You glared at me
I glared at you
And I glared at we,
But not deeply
Enough
Caught up in the rhythm and rhyme
The dreams he didn't find
Making me lose my mind
All because I ain't had none that week
Priorities need a tweak
Wasted all those months
Days and weeks
Only to become incomplete for underground
CD's and DVD's

A Song for the Blues

I remember the first we met
My heart was beatin' right out my chest
You looked at me and I looked at you
And we continue to do the things we do

Started dating, calling day and night
Then one day you ask me to be your wife
Never believed it could be like this
That my life could have so much bliss

'Cuz I got
Sugar lumps and black eye blues
Sugar lumps and black eye blues
Sugar lumps and black eye blues
That's what I got 'cuz I been messin' with you

Honeymoon, feeling so right
That's until we had our first fight
Should've known that it would come to this
'Cuz in his anger he throws the first fist

Promised he would never do me wrong
Became a mantra, same ol' song
Mama told me to leave this man
But loneliness kept my feet in the sand

'Cuz I got
Sugar lumps and black eye blues
Sugar lumps and black eye blues
Sugar lumps and black eye blues
That's what I got 'cuz I been messin' with you

Year went by, change in you
Acted like a jerk right down to the root
Quit your job, lazy man
Wallow 'round the house given me demands

Wish I'd seen this ugly beast
'Cuz I would have no to the priest
Your mom moved in, another sin
You just scratch your ass wearin' a grin

But there we were, sayin' our vows
And I remember screamin' out loud
My mind said "YES"
But my heart said "NO"
But I'm at the alter with nowhere to go

And I've got
Sugar lumps and black eye blues
Sugar lumps and black eye blues
Sugar lumps and black eye blues
That's what I got 'cuz I been messin' with you

Again, We

To die in your arms
is something already accomplished
Not bound to sequels
Found cliff hangered edge comforting
Slice vertical "I Love You's"
Wanting pin-drop remains to sound like the sweet nothings
never breathed during a pillowed evening
Bathed in electric embrace
Drank pilled forget-me-nots
hoping you'd find me slain by your neglect
But the movie neglected to show the part
Where you never showed...

To die in your arms
is something already accomplished
Not bound to sequels
Now can't
The movie didn't show the part
Where you never showed

Masked Salvation

Despondent
~~Slashed~~ and burned

Cut so deep
Bled the blood of other transferred revulsion
Wallow in pools of uncertainty
Suffering suffocates hopes and dreams
Made to feel inferior
Because of despair, find comfort in the silence
Silence speaks volumes
Sadness o o z e s from blades that provide temporary comfort
With each passing drop of blood,
The lancet plants its roots into my soul and blossoms
to slice away anguish
Each razor image is put to rest
As crimson stream flows into the evils
that support the discomfort that I feel

I have you to thank

Dessert

Servin' It Up and Thinkin' It Over

<u>You, I Like In Secret</u>

Like you in the middle of the day
Potent
Ripe for the risking
Sipping each to each
Nectar goggled
Ogling foreshadow
Post meridian pungent
Stint well spent

A Man in a Suit Is Dangerous

A man in a suit is dangerous
Decked out head to toe with teeth as white as new fallen snow
But hopefully, you plus me equals us

Want to be your only; melting into your hand
Pelvis thumping to rhythms of your heart; want you to know
A man in a suit is dangerous

Every night, swaddle me with your caress; staring at engagement band
Swallow fears of self-doubt; you make me glow
But hopefully, you plus me equals us

Dropped uncertainty; fell into your command
Couldn't help but fall in love with such a charming fellow
A man in a suit is dangerous

You make me leave my childhood on deserted sand
Escalating my maturity; never falling below
But hopefully, you plus me equals us

Want to landscape our future; let womb fertilize generations
Cascade through time; wherever you want to go
A man in a suit is dangerous
But hopefully, you plus me equals us

A Christmas Moment

Chris must
Chris must
Chris…

Must be crazy
If he thinks I will succumb to Chester colored nuts
Roasted and toasted under a pine tree
that scales roofs
Where Santa and eight tired as hell reindeer
settle to deliver gifts
[*kids know Target is the only elf that made their toys*]

Chris must
Chris must
Chris…

Must be crazy
If he thinks that in order to get out of meeting my parents
and getting me something meaningful
He's going to continue giving me sloppy kisses
under the mistletoe

Want U 2 Love Me

I want you love me like you
Don't love nobody else, I
Gave all my love to you so I
Don't have any for myself
Why, don't you notice that?
I'm dying over you

Love me the way that I am
'Cuz this is all I got
Tired of being second
Third
Fourth
Fifth
Sometimes not placed at all
Aren't I worthy of a remote section of your cerebellum?
What else do I have to do?
Might as well be alone
because treating me in this manner fucking blows
Want to grow my own dick
At least I know then
when I am being fucked over
You were supposed to be different
Sweeping me into a wishful bliss
Scrambling my life
Flipping me upside down
because you said that what love is
and that's what love does
But you didn't with me
Why the fuck not?
Can't you see that I am you're everything?
I'm the one that will wipe your snot when you're sick
Wash your ass when you can't
Feed your body and soul
when the world leaves you high and dry
Not because I have been told to
But as your lover I will do
But you didn't with me

Why the fuck not?
I've bent over backwards for you so much
I've got scoliosis
Worked my fingers to the bone slaving for you
Only to catch arthritis from your icy touch
Let your liquor filled lyrics poison me so badly
My heart is jaundiced
Only for you not to notice an damn thing
So why can't I shake you?
Like a moth to a flame continually burning from your existence
You and I both allowed me to do so
Falling captive to your absurdity
Time wasted and energy destroyed
A wall rebuilt
Love has become a chore you made for me
Indifference coated with your disputatious attitude
All I wanted to you to do is…

Love me, like you
Don't love nobody else, I
Gave all my love to you so I
Don't have any for myself
Why, don't you notice that?
I'm dying over you

Revealed: A Ballad

I smile…
because you said I should
I laugh…
because you told me to
I speak…
the way you ask me to
Yet I am not good enough for you

I wear the mask
Conceal my freedom
To live up to your expectations
A shadow of what I am destined to be
Wilting, before your very eyes
And you fail to see me
As you dish out demands
Never lending a helping hand

When I look to you
To make a pathway for myself
You deny me
Freedom
Smothering my dream
In the shadow of your wants

I smile…
because you said I should
I laugh…
because you told me to
I speak…
the way you ask me to
Yet I am not good enough for you

Onyx Dream

Love me
The only request that I have
The only thing that I'll ask
'cuz, it's you that I miss
and not just the kiss,
But the touch of your lips
when they touch mine
Listen to the truth that beats within my veins,
Pulsating synapses that you placed in me
You lit a fire
that won't simmer down
So,

Allow me to
Linger in all that is you
I want to you yearn for me as I
Eagerly await your presence
Satisfy my thirst by gulping
Handfuls of your charm; drowning me becoming you
Allow me to
Lick you to lullaby land
Illuminate your senses to
Energize your soul so you could
See me for what I am worth; tired of
Haggling your heartstrings, please
Allow me to
Lap up the doubts about us; massage negative
Impulses by masturbating your mind
Easing the tensions, so the juices in your brain
Secrete my name
Help me to, allow me to
And

Just love me
The only request that I have
The only thing that I'll ask
'cuz, it's you that I miss

and not just the kiss,
But the touch of your lips
when they touch mine
Listen to the truth that beats within my veins,
Pulsating synapses that you placed in me
You lit a fire
that won't simmer down
Love me

Help Me Hear Mermaids Singing

Witches' brew; frolic
Cackle and coo séanced tongue
At pagan pace, paw spirits through integument
Necromance me
Singed in salaciousness
Conjure dalliances befitting magnificent thirst
Entreat souls
Pray inside me
Enlace rosary and Hail Mary's choked wisdom
Soil remains in scriptured repentance
Baptize ecstasy
Secular secretions clear confusions
With scarlet affixed cross brows
Discover the lost art of veracity
Tell no one
Silence the wind
Yield from shattering bone
Fill fecund fissures in incantations
Beckon in breathed novelty
Tomb tainted tomes
Love noted in limited lettering
Spellbinding beginnings with back bending worship
Stimulate me anew

Some Happy Episodes

Remember
Gazing down bronze figure
Picturing moments when two become one
Painting essence with simple kisses
Watching night twinkle day
Eyes graze memories linked to senses of moments passed
Rekindle
Forward leaning into uncharted waters
Fingertips ripple honey dipped skin
Fondle as if mounting flags onto new territory
Pacing through plantation strands
Lovingly licking lavender lips
Cascade Hershey mountain peaks
Trot coca's flat lands
Slide into saccharine Nile
Hum tunes in chocolate prairie
Together spoke in love;
Lust and lavishness
We whisper lexis luxuriousness
Making tongue cum
Emotions surrender to pulsating arms and legs
Urges connecting pelvis to pelvis
Bust to thrust
Leaving what we must
Into synchronized pendulum wails
Heaving to leave wanting more
Cuddling thoughts
Senses
Memories and moments
Wanting more time to just
Remember

Music

Complicated
This melody can't be traced to one rhythmic beat
But catchy enough to entrance the soul
Excitingly peaceful
I want more
Love; not a powerful enough word
To describe emotions encamping spirit
Dance around to try to find the balance
Equality need not find this measure of music
Won't leave my mind
Smitten by musical intervals
Circling the visions seen
Want to capture them
Make a carbon copy for this joy that I feel
Sun rises and sets to complete the day
The melodic structure rocks me to sleep
Tender notes scale through satisfaction
Each octave tickling ebony's ivory
A symphony of untouchable beats
Lay in bed
Focused on this complicated melody
In hopes that it's repetitious

<u>Only You Can</u>

Eat
Me
Long
Time
Ravish
My
Body
Until
I
Am
So
Tender
That
I
Fall
Off
My
Own
Bones
Melting
Into
A
Puddle
Of
Myself

No Longer a Lazy Mind

Cathartic scribbling
Representing
Documenting
Forming
Legitimacy
Black canvassing the white with linear formations
Seeping into the pages
Wanting to devour all
Clawed writing instruments
Digging through the mounds of words
Penetrating deeper than deep
Sprung a leak
Of ink
Dripping from the palms
Fingertips oozing wisdom from the findings
Attached to the knowledge flowing from the un-dammed sheets
Married to images unanticipated
In love with the intelligibility
Wallowing in the juices created
When lexis linked to un-caged minds
Find the time to craft contemplation
Tangoing in the essence of astuteness
Giving birth to significance
This embryonic structure shall be named Infinite
Swaddling the notion of repetition
Escaping fallacy by thumbing notebook spine
Tickling it with ballpoint
Erecting more than words
Living by the thread of syntax

Life' Song

Spoon digging a concrete situation
Realizing that life ain't fair
Working hard to come up empty handed
And no one with knowledge to spare

Fighting wars with no reason
Explanations null and void
I vote but it does not matter because
My bush has no voice

What is air without freedom?
Stifled breath in a nation
Battling suffocation
I've got so much to learn

Searching for solace betwixt blank pages
Mentors seem to come and go
Flick through channels to find the answers
But media don't make news no more

Corporations got me hung by name brand
Making me believe that's what I need
All I want is what's owed to me
My words and the right to be free

Stop letting me live your lie
And letting my words slide by
I'm brighter than you let me shine
So, quit the madness
And remember this line

What is air without freedom?
Stifled breath in a nation
Battling suffocation
I've got so much to learn

Rambling Alphabetical

All the while loving you
Because I thought it was the right thing
Can't believe I fell into the hype
Despondency drowns my eyes
Eternally erasing hope
Fear enters, and forever lost because
God can't even erase my slate of
Hate clean
I am not strong enough to get caught up in the rapture of love
Jolted by the aftermath of ignorance and betrayal, I could
Kill that sorry excuse of human existence for
Leaving me alone when I started off that way
Melancholy
Never wanting this predicament but he wanted me to be
Open in more ways than one and I
Played that game for as long as I could
Quietly, submitting to my chocolate tyrant as he
Raped me of my sense of self and control
So, I got
Twisted up in his spell
Unknowingly, falling captive to this neurotic
Vile, son of a bitch
Well, I suppose it was my fault? Should have stuck with my
Xenophobic tendencies and
Yoked you when you tried to woo me with that sorry pick up line
Zilch...Lost...Love?

(only a tennis player can understand this shit)

76

Al Jebr

A love sautéed too long in melancholy melodies
Garnished with crisp calumniation
Rodger and Hammerstein dreams
Dipped in polite deception
Scores of hors d'oeuvres temporarily fill main course desires
Cunctation cocktails
Sweetly slipping sly soliloquies
Served thin veneers; sheer strips of coated façades
Eluded security
Broken maybes etch daylight;
dawning across shoulder blades;
china patterned nightmares gazing at repeat afflictions
Filet-ed and open faced
Contaminated for future lovers

Still Want It

A relationship is a RUT

Routinely yet Unconditionally Troubling
Requiring Understanding and Trust
Regret, Unforeseen passion and Turmoil
Regularly Undergoing Transition

And still want to be part of this foundation
Even though he touches the wrong places
Strokes in the wrong direction
(Should've known because he can't piss in the toilet)
But when he's drunk, I do like the way he works it
Because he works extra hard
And I work extra hard to love him

A relationship is a RUT

Regularly Undergoing Transition
Regret, Unforeseen passion and Turmoil
Requiring Understanding and Trust
Routinely yet Unconditionally Troubling

But I'd rather have something than nothing

Remission

Love
If you want to call it that
Fell off
Like a band aid
That over stayed its welcome
On a wound
That would soon be sensitive again
Love
If you want to call it that
Sparked
Like a friendship
Ignited into relationship that blew out
Abruptly
But not without secreting passion
Slithering down bend of neck
Arch of back
Cushion of belly
Crevice of pelvis
Coiling body in fictitious romance
Lethal injections of pain and pleasure
Obscuring thoughts of reason
Breaking miasma of lies
Mind whispers release
Lust with deeper tambour
Throbbing harder than logic
Ears drowning out the rustle of whines
Permitting physical chaos to manipulate truth
Weaving webs of nonsensical story line
Subscribing to fables
Delving into pages
Searching for answers
Cringing memory of wayward moments
A fool in lust
Poisoned truth
Clutching fallacies of "could be's"
Sniveling over "would be's" and "should be's"
Too busy fucking happenstance

Love
If you want to call it that
Never had a chance
Time to let go

OPEN LETTER TO THE LOVE OF MY LIFE
an epilogue
***

Every now and again
Daydream about the aroma of your heartbeat
Reminding muted flesh that it loved without question
Out of the blue one Thursday afternoon
Leave it to
Time's cruel tenacious
Trickery combined with
Our inability to voyeur future, we
Combust in a fiery of misunderstandings and
Simmered unrequited reliance
Eventually belly up in hope-in-stance;
unmoved stubborn assumptions of
Each other. Instead of loathing you for deserting me,
chose to believe that you
Loved me once
(*that which is much more savory than the bitter tinged sautéed
sorrows of missing the 'us' in 'u'*)

To a next time of do-overs...

Warmest Regards,

SNEAK PEAK
an excerpt from Confectionately Yours
***

You say my pen is dangerous
That's because you haven't stood in an alleyway at 2am
Listening to the gutter wails of a newborn
Craving substance from an abused milk duct of silence
Starving for everything it can't afford

You say my pen is dangerous
That's because you have never awoken to night terrors of enemy lines
Bullet stares of contradiction
Cradle rocking denial in slow beating purple hearts
Where drum majors rat-a-tat-tat on the fatigued misled

You say my pen is dangerous
That's because you've never held a conversation with the Black
Panther
Who sat in the last row; last seat
Where her "by any means necessary"
Necessarily meant she was never heard
Backpedaling swallowed afterthoughts
Her fringe was only décor for the movement

You say my pen is dangerous
That's because you've never been a cancer cell on a suicide mission
Holding a one way ticket to injustice on a body pleading for life
Where kitchen sink cocktails are the only in-flight meal
Before hitting the towers of mental destruction

You say my pen is dangerous
That's because you never watched the last episode of American Band
Stand; the one night the revolution was televised and integration swept
the nation
Displaying that prosperity could no longer be deferred
But the FCC pulled the plug on humanity
Suppose being an American is true genocide

You say my pen is dangerous…

ABOUT THE AUTHOR
***

When not sitting in front of the computer, Hawkins is performing and promoting literacy in public schools. She just finished a **Puppets and Poets** residency in New York with Alphabet Arts. This program spring boarded Hawkins out of her poetry bubble to produce "poem as play" and learn the basic fundamentals of puppetry. Her piece *Seeking Silence* received rave reviews from the audience and program directors. Additionally, she crafted a mini tour called the **Silent No More Tour** featuring her new work *Cartons of Ultrasounds*, where in each state, a new director, mask maker or puppeteer was added to bring a fresh concept to the same piece of text. Finding solace in the New York poetry scene Hawkins works as a judge/coach for **Poetry Out Loud**; an educational organization where young poets recite classic poems in slam competition form. Recently, she was featured in *Certain Circuits Magazine*, *Third Sunday Blog Carnival*, a CD compilation by Drexel University, and Lady M Productions CD *Arts4TheCause*. In addition, Hawkins released two of her own poetry albums, *Sugar Lumps and Black Eye Blues* and *Running Still Water*!

A Temple University **Poetry as Performance** alum, she has taken her skills outside the classroom and into the world. Since 2006, she has written five publications titled *Sugar Lumps and Black Eye Blues*, *Confectionately Yours*, *Mahogany Nectar* and *Lil Blæk Book: All the Long Stories Short* and *The Hotel Haikus*. Next to be released is *Black Suga: diary of a troublesome teenager* and *Poetry Schmo-etry* which will be poetry collections for children and teens. It is with hope that they will follow in the latter books' successes in print and radio media. Selections from her books have been featured at: BAX, 107.9 WRNB, Verseadelphia, LP Spoken Word Tour, Brown Girl Radio: a Cure for the Common, Da Block, WRTI 90.1 FM, Studio Luna, Improv Café, Temple University, PBGP, Aspire Arts, NBC 10, Moonstone: 100 Poets Reading, NateBrown Entertainment, The Liacouras Center, Tree House Books, The Bowery, Warmdaddy's, Jus Words, NJPAC, T Bar, Verbal Roots, The NAACP, The REC, Lyrical Playground, Lincoln University, The Pleazure Principle, Bar 13, Robin's Bookstore, umuvme Radio, First Person Arts, Drexel University, The

RED Lounge for AIDS Awareness, Women's Ink, Lady M Events, 6B Lounge, The Painted Bride, So 4Real, Charis Books, American Family Theater National Touring Ensemble, Authors Under 30 Book Tour, First Person Arts and Dr. Sonia Sanchez Literacy Night just to name a few.

Currently, she is the Producer/Host for her own radio show and owner of **HawkEye Entertainment, page2stage LLC**. On the horizon, Hawkins will be debut her new band, **Meredith & The Moonshine**; an all women of color country/bluegrass ensemble!

For bookings and detailed information:
www.TSPoetics.com